Lunchboxes

ANNABEL KARMEL

Lunchboxes

First published in Great Britain in 2003

1 3 5 7 9 10 8 6 4 2

Text © Annabel Karmel 2003
Photographs © William Lingwood 2003

First published by Ebury Press
Random House, 20 Vauxhall Bridge Road,
London SW1V 2SA

Random House Australia (Pty) Limited
20 Alfred Street, Milsons Point, Sydney,
New South Wales 2061, Australia

Random House New Zealand Limited
18 Poland Road, Glenfield, Auckland 10, New Zealand

Random House South Africa (Pty) Limited
Endulini, 5A Jubilee Road, Parktown 2193, South Africa

The Random House Group Limited Reg. No. 954009

www.randomhouse.co.uk

A CIP catalogue record for this book is available from the British Library.

Editor: Emma Callery
Designer: Ghost Design
Photographer: William Lingwood
Food stylist: Dagmar Vesely
Picture stylist: Helen Trent

ISBN 0091 888018
Papers used by Ebury Press are natural, recyclable products made from
wood grown in sustainable forests.
Printed and bound by Tien Wah in Singapore

Contents

The creative lunchbox

Welcome to Lunchboxes, the book aimed at putting the fun back into making packed lunches for children. The ubiquitous sandwich needn't be a piece of ham slammed between two pieces of bread, it can be a delicious moist filling of chopped ham and tomatoes mixed into cream cheese to fill a pitta pocket. Hot meals can warm a hungry tummy on cold winter days and treats can be made by your child to meet their own, sometimes exacting, needs.

Almost half the children in this country take a packed lunch to school, but making a packed lunch every day in the rush before school can become a real nightmare. It is estimated that 19.5 billion packed lunches are put together in the UK each year and, of these, 5.5 billion are for children. Packed lunches are often seen by parents as the healthier option, but in practical terms this is often wishful thinking.

- How do you make a packed lunch healthy and still get your child to eat it?
- What do you do if your child is a fussy eater and only likes peanut butter or jam sandwiches?
- How do you keep the food fresh and still looking good?
- How do you cope when other children bring in lunchboxes filled with crisps, chocolate biscuits and fizzy drinks?
- What do you do if you want your child to have a hot meal for lunch when it's cold and miserable weather?
Read on, that's what you do!

Food for your child's lunchbox

In a recent survey on children's packed lunches it was found that eight in ten packed lunches include crisps or savoury snacks (see below). Over a third of parents give a chocolate biscuit and almost three in ten a chocolate bar. However, fresh fruit is provided by over two-thirds of parents and virtually everyone includes a sandwich in their child's lunchbox.

Top ten items packed in children's lunchboxes
(Mintel Children's Packed Lunches report 2002)
1 Sandwich 94%
2 Crisps and snacks 84%
3 Fruit juice or juice drink 72%
4 Piece of fresh fruit 68%
5 Yoghurt/fromage frais 56%
6 Chocolate biscuit 35%
7 Cheese portion 31%
8 Chocolate bar 29%
9 Cake bars/slice of cake 26%
10 Cereal bar 25%

A healthy lunchbox should:
- Help to improve your child's attention, behaviour and learning in the afternoon.
- Provide one-third of your child's daily requirements of nutrients.
- Contain a source of protein to keep children alert, complex carbohydrates for slow release energy, protein and calcium for growth, fat for staying power, and fruit and vegetables for vitamins and minerals.

I'm not a believer in extremes of any kind – I don't think crisps or chocolate biscuits should be off limits to children in moderation, but neither do I believe that a jam sandwich, packet of crisps, chocolate bar and a fizzy drink constitutes a proper meal. There is a happy medium and it's important to remember that habits and food choices begin in childhood and what children eat can make a big difference to their long-term health.

Carbohydrates: choose complex carbohydrates like wholemeal bread, pasta, potatoes or rice. Pasta or rice salads make a nice change from sandwiches. Complex carbohydrates release calories slowly and help to keep up energy levels and concentration whereas refined carbohydrates like white bread, biscuits or cakes only provide instant, short-lived energy. They have also been stripped of their natural fibre during processing and have lost most of their valuable nutrients. The more fibre and protein is eaten alongside starchy or sugary foods, the more slowly those foods are digested and released as sugar into your system.

For fast release energy give: banana, dried fruit, apricot, mango, fruit juice, white bread, popcorn.

For slow-release energy give: pasta salad with tuna or chicken, peanut butter sandwich on wholemeal bread, egg sandwiches, rice cakes with hummus, pumpkin or sunflower seeds, nuts, raw vegetables and cherry tomatoes, apple, grapes, plums, kiwi fruit.

Calcium: children under the age of five shouldn't have a low fat diet so choose whole milk products like Greek yoghurt rather than low-fat yoghurt. In a recent survey it was found that 25% of young girls were eating too little calcium to build strong bones and this could lead to osteoporosis later in life, so make sure that you regularly include dairy products in your child's lunchbox. Cheese,

yoghurt, fromage frais, yoghurt drinks, smoothies and milkshakes are all excellent sources of calcium.

Fruit and vegetables: health experts recommend that we should try to include five portions of fruit and vegetables in our diet every day. Here is an idea of what counts as one portion:

- 1 medium-sized piece of fruit, e.g. apple, banana.
- A small bunch of grapes or 2 small fruits, e.g. apricots or a cupful of berries.
- 45 g (1½ oz) dried fruit.
- 1 serving of fruit salad or salad.
- 75 g (3 oz) cooked or raw vegetables.
- 1 glass fruit juice or fruit smoothie.

Different fruits and vegetables provide different vitamins and minerals so try to include a wide variety. It's a good idea to include a vitamin C-rich drink like orange juice or cranberry juice to help boost iron absorption. Choose unsweetened fruit juices or nutritious fruit smoothies. Dried fruits are also very nutritious. Raw vegetables with a dip and salads with a tasty dressing are popular ways to get your child to eat more vegetables.

Protein: some good sources of protein are chicken, tuna, egg, cheese and peanut butter and you can use these to make delicious sandwiches, pitta pockets or tortilla wraps. You can also make delicious pasta, rice or couscous salads with meat, chicken, fish or beans.

Fat: whilst it's true that young children need proportionately more fat in their diet than adults this should come mainly from nutritious foods like cheese, avocado and nuts. However, there's nothing wrong with including a treat like a muffin, cookie or crispy rice bar in your child's lunchbox.

Packing your child's lunchbox

- When choosing a lunchbox make sure that it is big enough to contain all the food your child needs but not so large than the food rattles around and your child has an unnecessarily large bag to carry. It's a good idea to choose an insulated box and one that will accommodate an ice pack to keep food fresh. Make sure you put your child's name on the lunchbox.
- There's nothing more stressful than trying to do too much in the morning and worrying that your child will be late for school. So it's a good idea to set out lunchboxes, plastic containers, napkins, utensils, etc., the night before. Pack up what you can like muffins, biscuits and fruit and make a list of the food you need to make and pack in the morning.
- Keep a good supply of cling film, foil, twist ties, sandwich bags, plastic spoons.
- It's worth buying a wide-mouthed vacuum flask, plastic sandwich-size containers to avoid squashed sandwiches, and other plastic containers for things like salads and cut-up fruit.
- Much of the food in a packed lunch is finger food but spoons, forks and knives do widen the range of foods that can be served. It's worth getting some colourful disposable plastic cutlery for your child.
- Be sure that lids are tight fitting and screwed on but also be sure that they can be opened by your child.
- Cut-up vegetables like carrot sticks can dry out so it's a good idea to wrap them in some damp kitchen paper to prevent this from happening.
- Dressings for most salads are best packed separately in small plastic pots otherwise salads can become quite soggy and limp.
- Next time you are in a fast food restaurant, save mini portions of ketchup, salad dressing, etc. They are always useful for your child's lunchbox.

Safety

- Think of all the foods that we commonly keep in the fridge: those are the foods that can spoil between the time your child leaves the house and the time he eats his packed lunch. Try to ensure they are kept cool.
- You can make sandwiches on frozen bread. The cold bread will help to keep the rest of the lunchbox cool and the bread will have thawed by lunchtime.
- It's a good idea to buy an insulated lunchbox. Lunchboxes left in a warm place can become a breeding ground for germs. To keep your child's lunchbox cool, buy a mini ice pack or freezer gel pack, which can be frozen and inserted with the lunch. Buy a couple of ice packs so that you will always have one in the freezer. Alternatively, freeze a carton or plastic bottle of juice overnight. The frozen drink will help keep food cool and will have defrosted by lunchtime.
- Sometimes one of the children in a child's class can have an allergy to peanuts. This can be very serious, in which case the school can insist that no child bring any products containing peanuts in their lunchbox.
- Test your child's vacuum flask to make sure it keeps food hot or cold. Some flasks that come with lunchboxes aren't very effective.
- It is a good idea to pack a small packet of wet wipes in the lunchbox so that your child can wipe his hands.

Getting children involved

- Take your child with you sometimes when you shop for food. If you can't take your child with you, then get him to make a list of foods that he would like you to buy.
- Try brainstorming some lunchbox ideas with your child and plan your child's lunchboxes two or three days ahead. Perhaps let your child look through this book and pick out a few new recipes to try each week.

- If your have the time, your child can help prepare some of the food that goes into his lunchbox. He could help make his own sandwiches or salads or make muffins, biscuits or crispy rice cakes at the weekend.
- Start a cookie cutter collection; there are some wonderful shapes to be found. Your child will enjoy cutting sandwiches into novelty shapes.

Small additions make life more interesting
There are some popular mini snacks now available in supermarkets, which are ideal for lunchboxes. Here are some ideas for you to try:
- Cheese strings.
- Miniature cheeses.
- Twin cartons of cream cheese with miniature breadsticks.
- Probiotic mini yoghurt drinks.
- Fromage frais or yoghurt in tubes or pouches.
- Mini packs of dried fruit or nuts and raisins.
- Vegetable crisps made from carrot, sweet potato, beetroot.
- Cereal and dried fruit bars (choose ones that are not loaded with sugar or fat).
- Yoghurt-covered raisins.
- Individual portions of fruit purée, e.g. apple purée or apple and strawberry.
- Nuts, provided there is no nut allergy in the family. Honey roasted cashew nuts are delicious.
- Dried fruit, e.g. dried apricots, figs, apples, mini packet of raisins.
- Pitta bread with hummus.
- Rice cakes, breadsticks, oatcakes.
- Homecooked popcorn.
- Twiglets.

Something hot
As the colder weather sets in it's a good idea to include something hot in a lunchbox. A wide-mouthed mini flask would be ideal for serving up a delicious cup of home-made or bought soup like a tomato, vegetable, chicken noodle or minestrone soup. Other good ideas for hot food in a vacuum flask are:
- Baked beans.
- Bolognese sauce with pasta.
- Chilli con carne.
- Stir-fried rice with chicken.

Encouraging your child to eat
Nutrition is important but, let's face it, it's parents rather than children who are concerned about the healthy aspect of food. However healthy the food is, it won't get eaten unless it's tasty and appealing to your child.

When your child brings his lunch to school, he carries a little piece of home with him. When my three children each had to take in lunchboxes it became a challenge to come up with something new to entice them to eat healthy food and bring a smile to their face after a long morning at school. Simple touches can make all the difference like cutting sandwiches into shapes using cookie cutters or threading fruit onto a straw to make fresh fruit skewers.

Variety is the spice of life and with a little effort there can be so much more to lunchboxes than sandwiches, crisps and chocolate biscuits. My aim with this book is to give parents lots of choices, ideas and inspiration to make really special lunchboxes for their child to enjoy while growing up, without spending long in the kitchen. You will find plenty of enticing recipes on the following pages.

Special sandwiches

Sandwiches don't need to be boring – try novelty-shaped, cut-out sandwiches, double-decker sandwiches, pitta pockets or tortilla wraps.

The perfect sandwich

There are so many different types of breads available now in the supermarket that can be used to make sandwiches. Try ciabatta, multi-grain or granary bread, mini pitta pockets, mini baguettes, raisin bread, bagels, rye or sun-dried tomato bread.

If you are usually in a rush in the morning, it will help if you get the ingredients together and make up your tuna or egg salad the night before.

To keep the sandwiches fresh, always wrap in cling film or silver foil as soon as you have made them.

To prevent sandwiches getting squashed, store them in a small plastic container in your child's lunchbox.

Start a cookie cutter collection. Cutting a sandwich into a fun shape like a teddy bear, heart or a car makes it much more exciting to eat. Older children will love to cut out the shapes themselves.

Keep a selection of breads in the freezer for emergencies. You can take out two slices of frozen bread in the morning to make a sandwich. It will thaw by lunchtime and is less likely to absorb the filling.

To avoid soggy sandwiches, make sure you use dry ingredients. It's important to wash lettuce but dry it before putting it into the sandwich. It may also be an idea to pack soggy ingredients separately. For example, sliced tomato can seep into bread, so either pack it

separately and let your child add it to his sandwich or put a layer of lettuce on top of the tomato.

You can encourage your child to eat brown bread by making 'mismatch' sandwiches from one slice of brown and one slice of white bread. Alternatively, buy 'whole white' sliced bread in the supermarket – this is white bread made using one-third wholemeal flour.

Favourite sandwich fillings

- Cream cheese and ...
  Cucumber, chives, smoked salmon, crushed pineapple, chopped dried apricots, raisins, banana with a squeeze of lemon and honey.

- Tuna and ...
  Sweetcorn, spring onion and mayonnaise, diced celery or cucumber and mayonnaise, chopped egg and mayonnaise, avocado and mayonnaise with a squeeze of lemon juice.

- Peanut butter and ...
  Sliced banana with or without honey, strawberry jam or redcurrant jelly, raisins, grated carrot, diced apple.

- Grated cheese and carrot with mayonnaise.
- Butter, Marmite and shredded lettuce.
- Chopped hard-boiled egg mixed with mayonnaise, a knob of margarine, snipped chives or salad cress, salt and pepper.
- Sliced Swiss cheese, cherry tomatoes and shredded lettuce.
- Grated Cheddar and mango chutney or pickle.
- Hummus mixed with grated carrot and thinly sliced cucumber.
- Hummus, diced tomato and chopped hard-boiled egg.

- Mashed sardines with tomato ketchup and thinly sliced cucumber.
- Tinned or fresh salmon with mayonnaise, tomato ketchup and cucumber or spring onion.
- Shredded chicken, chopped tomato, chopped hard-boiled egg, snipped chives, lettuce and mayonnaise.
- Roast chicken, sweetcorn and mayonnaise.
- Bacon, lettuce and tomato.
- Mayonnaise mixed with a little pesto tossed with shredded chicken and salad.
- Sliced turkey or ham, Swiss cheese, tomato, cucumber and alfalfa sprouts with a little salad cream or mayonnaise.
- Roast beef, lettuce, pickled cucumber, tomato and a little mild horseradish or mustard.
- Ham, diced pineapple and cottage cheese.
- Bacon, lettuce, tomato and mayonnaise.
- Coronation chicken (see page 14).

To help you on your way
- Keep a supply of frozen bread, rolls, bagels, pitta bread, etc., in the freezer for emergencies.
- To save time, sandwiches can be prepared in advance and frozen without becoming soggy.

Foods that freeze well include: sliced meat, chicken, fish, cheese spreads and peanut butter.
Foods that do not freeze well include: hard-boiled egg whites, mayonnaise and salad dressing.

Don't add lettuce, tomatoes, cucumber, carrots or other raw vegetables before freezing – these could be packed separately and added to the sandwich just before eating. Wrap the sandwiches in freezer wrap and make sure that it is well sealed. Label and date each sandwich and use within two weeks.

Quick & yummy sandwich fillings

Prawn & watercress with tomato mayonnaise
4 slices granary bread
soft margarine or softened butter
a handful of watercress, trimmed
100 g (4 oz) prawns
2 tbsp mayonnaise
1 tbsp tomato ketchup
1 tomato, de-seeded and diced (optional)

Spread two slices of bread with margarine or butter and arrange the watercress on the bread. Mix the prawns together with the mayonnaise and ketchup, mix in the chopped tomato (if using) and spoon onto the watercress. Sandwich together with the remaining bread, cut into quarters and trim the crusts.

Coronation chicken

Coronation chicken has a delicious flavour and will keep for several days in the fridge. It makes a great sandwich filling with some crisp lettuce between the slices of bread or rolled up inside a mini tortilla or in a pitta pocket. Coronation chicken can also be served as a salad with rice, popped into a plastic container and packed up with the rest of the lunchbox.

Makes 4 portions
100 g (4 oz) basmati rice
½ chicken stock cube, dissolved in 300 ml (½ pint) boiling water
1 bay leaf
2 chicken breasts, cut into bite-sized chunks
1 tbsp vegetable oil
1 small onion, peeled and finely chopped
1 tsp medium curry powder
1½ tbsp mango chutney
1½ tbsp lemon juice
½ tbsp tomato purée
100 ml (4 fl oz) mayonnaise
75 ml (3 fl oz) mild natural yoghurt
fruit, e.g. seedless grapes or chopped mango

Cook the rice according to the packet instructions or alternatively use cooked rice.

Put the chicken stock into a saucepan together with the bay leaf. Bring to the boil then reduce the heat and poach the chicken for about 6 minutes. Leave the chicken in the stock to cool down.

Heat the oil in another saucepan, add the chopped onion and sauté for 2 minutes. Stir in the curry powder and cook for 30 seconds. Stir in the mango chutney, lemon juice, tomato purée and 100 ml (3½ fl oz) of the chicken stock. Simmer for 10 minutes. Strain through a sieve and allow to cool.

Mix together with the mayonnaise and the yoghurt and then mix in the chicken and fruit (if using).

Tuna & tomato

75 g can tuna or salmon, drained
1 tsp soft margarine or softened butter
1 tbsp tomato ketchup
1 tbsp mayonnaise
40 g (1½ oz) cucumber, diced
1 spring onion, finely sliced

Flake the tuna or salmon with a fork. Add the margarine or butter, tomato ketchup and mayonnaise and stir in the cucumber and spring onion.

Club sandwich

2 slices wholemeal bread
soft margarine or softened butter
a few crisp lettuce leaves
2 slices chicken breast
2 slices crisp bacon
2 slices tomato
mayonnaise

Spread the bread with butter or margarine. Lay the lettuce over the bread. Arrange the sliced chicken, bacon, tomato and a little mayonnaise on one slice of the bread. Then cover with some lettuce and, finally, the other slice of bread. Cut the sandwich in half and wrap tightly in cling film or foil.

Ricotta with apricots & honey

75 g (3 oz) ricotta
1 tsp runny honey
3 ready-to-eat dried apricots, chopped

Mix together the ricotta and honey and stir in the chopped apricots.

Roast beef

Pastrami on rye bread makes a good combination and, with some small additions like lettuce and mustard, it becomes an even better sandwich.

2 slices bread
soft margarine or softened butter
2 crisp lettuce leaves
2 slices rare lean roast beef or pastrami
horseradish or mustard
pickled cucumber

Spread the bread with butter or margarine, lay the lettuce over the bread and cover with the roast beef or pastrami, a little horseradish or mustard and a few slices of pickled cucumber. Cover with the remaining slice of bread and cut into two triangles.

Chicken & egg double-decker

2 slices white bread
1 slice brown bread

Egg mayonnaise
1 hard-boiled egg
½ tsp soft margarine
1½ tsp mayonnaise

2 tbsp salad cress
pinch paprika
salt and freshly ground black pepper

Chicken & tomato
1 tomato, thinly sliced into 4
40 g (1½ oz) cooked chicken, shredded
1 tsp mayonnaise

To make the egg mayonnaise, chop the hard-boiled egg and mix together with the margarine and mayonnaise. Stir in the salad cress and sprinkle with paprika.

Spread two slices of white bread with butter or margarine on one side and spread a slice of brown bread with butter on both sides. Cover one slice of the white bread with the egg mayonnaise and top with the brown bread.

To make the chicken filling, arrange the sliced tomatoes on top of the brown bread. Mix the shredded chicken together with the mayonnaise, spread over the tomatoes and top with the remaining slice of white bread.

With a sharp knife, trim off the crusts and cut into three strips. Wrap in cling film.

Other double-decker fillings to try:
- Mashed sardines with ketchup/cream cheese and cucumber.
- Chopped hard-boiled egg with salad cream/tuna mayonnaise, sweetcorn and spring onion.
- Smoked salmon/cream cheese and chive.
- Ham/sliced cheese and pickle.
- Ham/ricotta with honey and apricot (see above).
- Peanut butter and sliced banana/strawberry jam.

SPECIAL SANDWICHES

Classic BLT

There is something completely addictive about the combination of bacon, lettuce and tomato – a classic sandwich filling indeed.

4 rashers streaky bacon
2 slices granary bread
soft margarine or softened butter
a few crisp lettuce leaves
1 small tomato, sliced
mayonnaise

Grill the rashers of bacon until well cooked. Spread the bread with butter or margarine. Lay the lettuce leaves over the bread and cover with the sliced tomato and add a little mayonnaise. Chop the bacon rashers and scatter evenly over the tomatoes. Cover the bacon with the remaining slice of bread. Press together gently and cut into two triangles.

Ham & cheese

2 slices bread
soft margarine or softened butter
1 large thin slice Swiss cheese
1 slice turkey or smoked ham
4 thin slices cucumber
2 slices tomato
salt and freshly ground black pepper
1 tbsp mayonnaise

Butter the bread, arrange the cheese, ham, cucumber and tomato on top and season with a little salt and pepper. Add a blob of mayonnaise and cover with the remaining slice of bread. Remove the crusts with a sharp knife and cut into two triangles.

Baguette fillings

Mini baguettes are popular and can have savoury or sweet fillings (see the photograph on page 10). Here are my favourites, which are all quick to make when coping with that morning rush. They are also great fillings for sandwiches. The smoked salmon and cream cheese mix is also yummy on bagels (see opposite), and the tuna mix is perfect in pitta bread on spread onto a tortilla, which is then rolled up and wrapped with cling film.

Tuna with tomatoes & sweetcorn

105 g can tuna in oil, drained
2 tbsp mayonnaise
1 tbsp tomato ketchup
4 sunblush tomatoes, chopped
1 spring onion finely sliced
25 g (1 oz) sweetcorn

Flake the tuna with a fork and mix together with the mayonnaise and ketchup. Stir in the sunblush tomatoes, spring onion and sweetcorn.

Smoked salmon & cream cheese

2 tbsp cream cheese
½ tsp snipped chives
2 slices bread
a few slices cucumber (optional)
50 g (2 oz) sliced smoked salmon
squeeze of lemon juice
freshly ground black pepper (optional)

Mix together the cream cheese and chives and spread over the bread, lay the sliced cucumber (if using) and smoked salmon on top and squeeze over a little lemon juice. Finish with a grind of black pepper, if using.

Egg & cress

2 small eggs
2 tbsp mayonnaise
a knob of soft margarine or butter
salt and freshly ground black pepper
½ punnet mustard and cress

Put the eggs in a saucepan of cold water and bring to the boil. Reduce the heat and simmer for 7–8 minutes (the yolk should be solid). Drain the eggs and cool them under cold water. Peel the eggs when cold. Chop the eggs and put in a bowl together with the mayonnaise, margarine or butter, salt and pepper and mix well. Finally stir in the salad cress.

Peanut butter, jelly & banana

1 heaped tbsp peanut butter
1 tbsp redcurrant jelly, strawberry or raspberry jam
1 small ripe banana, sliced

Spread the peanut butter over one side of the baguette. Spread the redcurrant jelly, strawberry or raspberry jam over the peanut butter and top with the sliced banana.

Bagel fillings

Bagels are a perfect alternative to slices of bread or baguettes. They taste delicious, are a handy size – and make an unusual change. Try some of these fillings:

- Diced ham or chicken with chopped pineapple chunks and mayonnaise.
- Marmite and butter.
- Chopped hard-boiled egg and sandwich spread.
- Sliced turkey, Swiss cheese, tomato, salad and salad dressing or mayonnaise.

Chicken & sunblush tomato

1 tbsp cream cheese
½ tsp red pesto
1 sunblush tomato, chopped
15 g (½ oz) cooked chicken or turkey, chopped
1 bagel
a little shredded lettuce

Mix together the cream cheese and pesto and stir in the sunblush tomato and chicken. Slice the bagel in half horizontally, spread the base with the cream cheese and chicken mix and top with some shredded lettuce.

Stuffed pitta pocket with tuna, egg & sweetcorn

Stuffed pitta pockets with a nutritious filling make a good snack or light lunch. This tuna mix is delicious.

Makes 4 pitta pockets
2 eggs
200 g can tuna in oil, drained
100 g (4 oz) sweetcorn
2 tbsp mayonnaise
1 tsp white wine vinegar
4 spring onions, chopped
salt and freshly ground black
    pepper
a few drops Tabasco sauce
salad cress (optional)
2 pitta breads

Put the eggs in a saucepan of cold water and bring to the boil. Reduce the heat and simmer for 7–8 minutes (the yolk should be solid). Drain and cool under cold water. Peel the eggs when cold.

Meanwhile, flake the tuna with a fork and mix with the sweetcorn, mayonnaise, white wine vinegar, spring onions, salt and pepper and the Tabasco sauce. Roughly chop the hard-boiled eggs and add to the tuna mix with the salad cress (if using), stirring well.

Cut the pitta breads in half to give 4 pitta pockets and divide the mixture between them.

Lunchbox lowdown
• Add a personal touch to your child's lunch. Tuck in a note, stickers or joke or send a special treat labelled 'share with a friend'. Pack fun napkins, decorate lunch bags with stickers, draw a face on a banana with a marker pen.

Tortilla roll-ups

Makes 2 tortillas
½ tbsp olive oil
1 chicken breast, cut into strips
40 g (1½ oz) red onion, thinly sliced
1 small clove garlic, crushed
1 tsp balsamic vinegar
pinch oregano
salt and freshly ground black pepper
6 small cherry tomatoes, cut into quarters
4 sunblush tomatoes, chopped
3 basil leaves, torn into pieces
a drizzle of olive oil
freshly ground black pepper
2 large flour tortillas
mayonnaise
a little shredded iceberg

Heat the oil in a small frying pan and sauté the chicken, red onion and garlic for about 3 minutes. Add the balsamic vinegar, oregano and season to taste.

Meanwhile, mix together the cherry tomatoes, sunblush tomatoes and basil, drizzle over the olive oil and add a pinch of black pepper.

Spread the tortillas with a little mayonnaise. Divide the chicken and tomato mixture between the two tortillas and top with some shredded lettuce. Roll up the tortillas and wrap tightly in cling film.

Quick turkey wrap

Wraps make a great alternative to sandwiches and you can find soft flour tortillas in the bread section of most supermarkets. It's best to warm the tortilla in the microwave for a few seconds before filling as this makes the wrap more pliable. Other good tortilla fillings are:
- Tuna with sweetcorn, cucumber and mayonnaise.
- Chicken, avocado, salad and mayonnaise with toasted pine nuts.

Makes 2 tortillas
2 small flour tortillas (15 cm/6 in)
1 tbsp salad cream or mayonnaise
2 thin slices of turkey
a handful of shredded lettuce
2 heaped tbsp grated cheese

Lay out the tortillas, spread with salad cream or mayonnaise. Lay a turkey slice on top of each tortilla and cover with some shredded lettuce and grated cheese and roll up. Wrap with cling film.

Lunchbox lowdown
- Some 45% of pupils say they prefer to have a packed lunch to a school meal. If your child is a fussy eater, it can be much better to give him a packed lunch containing the food he likes rather than let him go hungry because he doesn't like school lunches.

Savoury specialities

If you pack a vacuum flask in your child's lunchbox you can give your child something hot like soup or pasta on a cold winter's day.

Home-made tomato soup

Home-made tomato soup is a favourite with everyone and this one is particularly delicious.

Makes 5 portions
Suitable for freezing
1½ tbsp olive oil
1 onion, chopped
2 carrots, peeled and chopped
400 g can chopped tomatoes
1 tbsp tomato purée
2 tsp garlic purée
½ tsp caster sugar
300 ml (½ pint) vegetable or chicken stock
bay leaf
salt and freshly ground black pepper
3 tbsp double cream (optional)
2 tbsp torn fresh basil leaves (optional)

Warm the olive oil in a saucepan over a low heat, then add the onion and carrots and sauté for 5 minutes. Add the remaining ingredients apart from the cream and basil. Bring to the boil, then cover and simmer for 20 minutes. Transfer to a blender and liquidise until smooth. Then return the soup to the pan, add the cream and basil (if using) and reheat. If your child doesn't like green bits floating around in the soup, you can leave out the basil.

Lunchbox lowdown
- To improve heat retention, rinse a vacuum flask with hot water before pouring in a hot soup.
- Freeze any of the soups given on these pages in individual containers. Then defrost a portion overnight, heat up in the morning and pour into a vacuum flask to keep it hot until lunchtime.

Minestrone soup with haricot beans

Haricot beans are rich in protein, vitamins and minerals. An alternative is baked beans.

Makes 8–10 portions
Suitable for freezing
2 tbsp olive oil
1 carrot, peeled and finely diced
1 stick celery, finely diced
1 red onion, peeled and finely diced
1 clove garlic, crushed
5 ripe plum tomatoes, peeled, seeded and roughly chopped (or 1 x 400 g can chopped plum tomatoes)
1 tbsp tomato purée
2.3 litres (4 pints) chicken stock
150 g (5 oz) green cabbage, finely sliced
8 basil leaves, torn into pieces
50 g (2 oz) small pasta shapes or spaghetti, broken into pieces
415 g can haricot or baked beans
salt and freshly ground black pepper
grated Parmesan cheese, to serve

Heat the olive oil in a large saucepan. Add the carrot, celery, onion and garlic and sauté for 10 minutes, stirring occasionally. Add the tomatoes, tomato purée and stock, bring to the simmer and cook for 15 minutes.

Stir in the cabbage, basil, pasta and beans and simmer for 15–18 minutes until the pasta is tender. Season and serve with grated Parmesan, packed in a separate small container for your child to add at lunchtime.

Sweet & sour chicken noodles

See the photograph on page 22.

Makes 2 portions
Sauce

1 tsp red wine vinegar
1 tbsp soy sauce
1 tbsp tomato ketchup
2 tbsp pineapple juice
½ tsp caster sugar
1 tsp cornflour

1 tbsp vegetable oil
100 g (4 oz) chicken
    breast, cut into strips
salt and freshly ground
    black pepper

2 tbsp finely sliced spring
    onion
50 g (2 oz) baby
    sweetcorn, sliced in half
    lengthways and then
    again widthways
1 carrot, peeled and cut
    into matchsticks
25 g (1 oz) French beans,
    topped and tailed and
    cut in half
50 g (2 oz) Chinese thread
    noodles

For the sauce, mix together all the ingredients and set aside. Heat half the oil in a wok or frying pan, lightly season the chicken and sauté for 3–4 minutes or until cooked through. Remove from the pan.

Add the remaining oil and stir-fry the vegetables for about 3 minutes. Pour over the sauce, bring to the boil, then reduce the heat and cook for 1 minute.

Cook the noodles according to the packet instructions, drain and mix together with the chicken and vegetables.

Chicken chunks on a stick

You can make these for dinner and wrap a couple of bamboo skewers in foil for your child's lunchbox the next day. For safety reasons, you might prefer to remove the food from the skewer before putting in the lunchbox – not such fun to eat, but better than an accident with the stick.

Makes 4 sticks

2 tbsp soy sauce
20 g (¾ oz) light
    muscovado sugar or
    soft brown sugar
1 tbsp lime or lemon juice

½ tbsp vegetable oil
1 small garlic clove,
    crushed
2 chicken breasts, cut into
    chunks

Put the soy sauce and sugar into a small saucepan and gently heat, stirring until the sugar has dissolved. Remove from the heat and stir in the lime juice, vegetable oil and garlic. Marinate the chicken for at least 1 hour or overnight.

Soak four bamboo skewers in water. Thread the chunks of chicken onto the skewers, place on a grill pan, brush with the marinade and cook under a pre-heated grill for 4–5 minutes each side, basting occasionally with the marinade until cooked through.

Finger-picking chicken balls

The grated apple adds a delicious flavour to these chicken balls and they are very popular eaten cold or hot. Include a little tomato ketchup in a separate plastic container for dipping the balls into.

Makes 20 chicken balls
Suitable for freezing

1 large Granny Smith
　apple, peeled and grated
2 large chicken breasts,
　cut into chunks
1 onion, peeled and finely
　chopped
1 tbsp chopped parsley
1 tsp fresh or ½ tsp
　dried thyme (optional)

50 g (2 oz) fresh white
　breadcrumbs
1 chicken stock cube,
　dissolved in 1 tbsp
　boiling water
salt and freshly ground
　black pepper
flour for coating
vegetable oil for frying

Using your hands, squeeze out a little excess liquid from the grated apple. Mix the grated apple with the chicken, onion, parsley, thyme leaves (if using), breadcrumbs and the dissolved chicken stock cube and roughly chop in a food processor for a few seconds. Season with a little salt and pepper.

With your hands, form the mixture into about 20 balls, roll in flour and fry in shallow oil until lightly golden and cooked through (about 10 minutes).

Sticky drumsticks

This tasty marinade gives drumsticks a delicious flavour. They can be marinated and cooked the day before and refrigerated. Halve the quantity of marinade for two drumsticks. Wrap the drumsticks in cling film or foil.

Makes 4 drumsticks

3 tbsp plum jam
1 tbsp soy sauce
1 tsp lemon juice

a few drops Tabasco
　sauce
1 tbsp sesame seeds
4 chicken drumsticks,
　skinned

Mix together the jam, soy sauce, lemon juice, Tabasco sauce and sesame seeds in a bowl. Score the drumsticks several times and mix into the marinade. Leave for 1–2 hours or overnight in the fridge. Pre-heat the grill to medium and place the chicken and marinade on a baking tray. Grill the chicken for about 20 minutes, basting with the marinade every 5 minutes and turning occasionally to prevent burning.

Lunchbox lowdown
- Put extra foil around the ends of chicken drumsticks so that your child can hold them without getting sticky fingers.
- Children tend to consume too much salt in their diet and high levels of salt can make them vulnerable to health problems like high blood pressure, heart disease and strokes. Many of the foods manufactured especially for lunchboxes like cheese strings, processed ham and cheese lunch packs, and salt and vinegar crisps are very high in salt. Check the label and avoid foods that have a high sodium content. Eating foods that contain potassium helps balance the effect of salt in the body. Bananas and dried apricots are a good source of potassium.

SAVOURY SPECIALITIES

Mini muffin pizzas

You can use whatever toppings your child likes for these mini pizzas. Try any of the following ideas: ham and pineapple, tuna and sweetcorn or cherry tomato and pepperoni. You can also make simple pizzas by spreading the muffins with tomato sauce, arranging sliced cherry tomatoes on top and then covering with grated Cheddar and cooking under the grill until lightly golden.

Makes 2 mini muffins

1 English breakfast muffin, cut in half
1 tbsp tomato purée
1 tsp red pesto
1 tbsp olive oil
½ small red onion, peeled and sliced
2–3 button mushrooms, sliced
½ small courgette, thinly sliced
Salt and freshly ground black pepper
1 slice ham or salami, cut into pieces (optional)
50 g (2 oz) grated Mozzarella or Cheddar cheese

Toast the muffin until golden and leave to cool. Pre-heat the grill to high. Mix the tomato purée and red pesto and spread over the muffins. Heat the olive oil in a frying pan and cook the onion, mushrooms and courgette until softened and golden.

Add seasoning and then divide the vegetables between the two muffin halves and scatter the ham or salami and Mozzarella or Cheddar cheese over the top. Place under the grill and cook for 4 minutes or until golden and bubbling. Leave to cool and wrap in cling film or foil.

Tortilla chips

It's easy to make your own tasty tortilla chips and they will keep fresh for a week if they are stored in an airtight container.

Makes as many as you want
Tortillas
Olive oil

Toppings
Grated Parmesan cheese
Sesame seeds
Poppy seeds
Fresh or dried herbs

Pre-heat the oven to 200°C/400°F/Gas 6.

Cut the tortillas into triangles approximately 6 cm (2½ in) high. Brush on both sides with olive oil and sprinkle with one or more of the toppings. Bake in the oven for 10 minutes, leave to cool on a metal rack and then transfer to an airtight container.

Lunchbox lowdown
- Send your child to school with a handful of these tortilla chips in a small plastic container and a dip like hummus or cream cheese and chives in a second container and some sticks of raw vegetables. An appetising and healthy lunchbox combination.
- If your child is always starving after school and can't wait to get home and have something to eat, pack a snack for after school in the lunchbox. Choose something that will not spoil like a tuna pitta pocket or peanut butter sandwich, a muffin, cereal bar or fruit.

SAVOURY SPECIALITIES

Spanish omelette with new potato, courgette & tomato

Spanish omelettes are good eaten hot or cold. You could cook this for your own supper and then wrap a piece up in foil and store in the fridge ready for your child's lunchbox the next day.

Makes 6 portions
100 g (4 oz) new potatoes
1 tbsp olive oil
1 small onion, peeled and
   finely chopped
1 courgette, diced or grated
2 tomatoes, skinned, de-seeded
   and roughly chopped
4 eggs
1 tbsp milk
2 tbsp freshly grated
   Parmesan cheese
salt and freshly ground
   black pepper

Bring a lightly salted saucepan of water to the boil, add the new potatoes, reduce the pan to a simmer and cook the potatoes for about 12 minutes, until tender. Drain, leave to cool and then cut into slices.

Heat the oil in an 18–20 cm (7–8 in) diameter non-stick frying pan. Add the onion and sauté for 2 minutes. Add the diced courgette and sauté for about 6 minutes. If using grated courgette, you will only need to cook the courgette for about 4 minutes. When the courgette is cooked, add the tomatoes and cook for 2 minutes, then stir in the sliced new potatoes.

Beat the eggs together with the milk, Parmesan cheese and a little seasoning. Pour the egg mixture over the vegetables and cook over a medium heat for about 4 minutes or until the eggs are set underneath. Meanwhile, pre-heat the grill to high. Place the frying pan under the grill (if necessary, wrap the handle with foil to prevent it burning) and cook for about 3 minutes, until golden and set. When the omelette is cold, cut into wedges and wrap in foil.

Lunchbox lowdown
• Girls start their growth spurt between the ages of 8 and 10 and boys start their growth spurt a little later, around the age of 12 years. Peak bone growth occurs around the age of 12 in girls and around the age of 14 in boys. Children between the ages of 7 and 12 should be drinking two-thirds of a pint of milk a day. One pot of yoghurt and 25 g (1 oz) hard cheese provide the same amount of calcium as one-third of a pint of milk.

Luscious lunch on a stick

You can make up 'kebabs', using straws instead of sticks, with many different foods. They are quick to put together and easy to pack in your lunchbox. Pack a pot of ketchup or a dip for added flavour. Here are some ideas for you to try but feel free to make up your own combinations choosing healthy foods that your child enjoys.

Try any of these suggestions for food combinations to thread onto your straws. There is plenty of scope for your children to help with this task.

- Slices of ham or turkey rolled up and interspersed with cubes of cheese and wedges of pineapple.
- Cherry tomatoes and chunks of cucumber and Mozzarella cheese.
- Slices of cooked sausages and gherkins.
- Pieces of carrot, celery, cucumber, red pepper and baby sweetcorn.
- Squares of Spanish omelette (see page 32).
- Salami, cubes of Mozzarella cheese and cherry tomatoes.

Honey & soy toasted seeds

These are very nutritious and taste wonderful. Sunflower seeds are a good source of the antioxidant vitamin E, which boosts the immune system and is vital for healthy brain function. Pumpkin seeds contain omega-3 fatty acids, which are crucial for brain development. They will keep for two weeks in an airtight container.

Makes 4 portions
1 tbsp sunflower oil
75 g (3 oz) sunflower
   seeds
75 g (3 oz) pumpkin seeds
1 tbsp runny honey
1 tbsp soy sauce

Heat the oil in a non-stick frying pan, add the seeds and cook, continuously stirring, for about 2 minutes or until the seeds are lightly browned. Remove from the heat, add the honey and soy sauce, return to the heat for 1 minute and then leave to cool.

Lunchbox lowdown
- To keep your child's lunchbox exciting, pack little surprises in it from time to time like stickers, a novelty pen, rubber or sharpener, mini notebook or a joke. Simple gestures like this will let your child know that your thoughts are with her, even when she is at school.

SAVOURY SPECIALITIES

Hidden vegetable tomato sauce

This delicious tomato sauce flavoured with Mascarpone cheese is a great way to get children to eat vegetables because the sauce makes them invisible and what they can't see, they can't pick out. You can leave out the Mascarpone if you prefer.

Heat the oil in a saucepan and sauté the onion for about 4 minutes. Add the carrot and red pepper and cook for 3 minutes. Add the courgette, passata, stock and sugar and simmer, covered, for 20 minutes. Add the balsamic vinegar and oregano and continue to cook for 5 minutes.

Meanwhile, cook the pasta according to the packet instructions.

Transfer the sauce to a food processor and blend until smooth. Return to the saucepan, add the Mascarpone cheese and gently heat, continuously stirring, until the cheese has melted into the sauce. Mix with the pasta and transfer one portion to a warmed vacuum flask.

Makes 5 portions
Sauce suitable for freezing

1 tbsp olive oil
½ red onion, peeled and chopped
2 carrots, peeled and grated
½ small red pepper, cored, de-seeded and chopped
1 small courgette, chopped
500 ml (16 fl oz) passata
125 ml (4 fl oz) vegetable stock
1 tsp sugar
1 tsp balsamic vinegar
1 tsp dried oregano
350 g (12 oz) pasta
100 g (4 oz) Mascarpone cheese

Lunchbox lowdown
• You can control what goes into your child's lunchbox but you can't control what goes into your child. I know it may seem obvious but make sure that you send your child to school with food that he likes. It's often a good idea, time permitting, to let your child get involved helping to pack his own lunchbox or perhaps discuss with him the night before what he would like to include.

SAVOURY SPECIALITIES

Crunchy salads

Instead of sandwiches, try making tasty pasta, rice or couscous salads for your child's lunchbox. The secret of getting your child to enjoy eating salad is to find an irresistible salad dressing – there are some fabulous dressings in this chapter.

Chicken Caesar salad

The croutons and dressing for this salad can be made the night before. Then all you need to do in the morning is sauté the chicken, mix all the ingredients together and toss with the dressing (see the photograph on the previous page). You could even use ready-made croutons and cooked chicken breast, in which case all you need to do is assemble all the ingredients – so simple!

Makes 1 portion

1 tbsp olive oil
1 slice thick white bread, crusts trimmed and cut into small cubes
1 chicken breast
1 baby gem lettuce or ½ Cos or romaine lettuce, cut into pieces
1 tbsp grated Parmesan cheese

Dressing

2 tbsp mayonnaise
1 tsp lemon juice
½ small clove garlic, crushed
⅛ tsp Dijon mustard
a few drops Worcestershire sauce
a few drops Tabasco sauce

Heat the olive oil in a small non-stick frying pan and add the cubes of bread. Fry, turning occasionally, until golden brown. Remove with a slotted spoon and drain on kitchen paper.

Cut the chicken into bite-sized pieces and add to the pan. Fry for 3–4 minutes until cooked through and leave to cool.

Mix together all of the dressing ingredients. Mix together the lettuce and chicken and toss with most of the dressing. Pack the grated Parmesan cheese and the croutons in a small separate plastic container for your child to scatter over the salad at lunchtime.

Lunchbox lowdown
- If your child likes to trade or share at lunchtime, include an extra 'valuable' treat like crispy rice squares, chocolate muffins or popcorn – you could label it 'For a Friend' if you like.

Pasta salad with Annabel's dressing

The secret of getting your child to eat salad is to find an irresistible dressing. This one is pure magic and I can't make enough of it to please my children. They love it – not only as a salad dressing but also on rice, chicken and pasta and as a dip with raw vegetables like sticks of cucumber, carrot and red pepper. I usually make up a large batch of the dressing and keep it in a bottle in the fridge.

To make the dressing, combine all the ingredients in a food processor and blend them until they are smooth.

Bring a saucepan of lightly salted water to the boil and cook the pasta according to the packet instructions.

Meanwhile, prepare the vegetables. Peel and cut the carrot into thin strips; top and tail the French beans, and chop the cherry tomatoes in half. If you are using frozen sweetcorn, cook it either in a saucepan of boiling water or in the microwave. Dice the chicken breast.

Put the carrot and French beans in a steamer (a two-tiered steamer would be good) for about 5 minutes or until tender but still crisp. Drain the pasta and mix it together with the carrot, French beans, tomatoes, sweetcorn and diced chicken. Toss with 100 ml (3½ fl oz) of the salad dressing.

Makes 4 portions
Dressing
½ small onion, peeled and finely
    chopped
4 tbsp vegetable oil
1½ tbsp rice wine vinegar
1 tbsp soy sauce
1 tbsp chopped celery
¼ tbsp finely chopped
    root ginger
1 tbsp water
1½ tsp tomato purée
1½ tsp caster sugar
1½ tsp lemon juice
salt and freshly ground
    black pepper

150 g (5 oz) pasta shapes
1 carrot
75 g (3 oz) fine French beans
6 small cherry tomatoes
100 g (4 oz) sweetcorn
1 small cooked chicken breast

Lunchbox lowdown
• Some schools operate a healthy eating policy with regard to packed lunches. For example, they might ban crisps or chocolate. It might be an idea to discuss this with some of the other parents and suggest a trial at your school.

Pasta with prawns & avocado

A prawn cocktail with a difference. If your child doesn't like avocado, leave it out and you could use chopped or cherry tomatoes instead.

Makes 3 portions

200 g (7 oz) pasta shapes
1 ripe avocado, chopped into 1 cm (½ in) cubes
200 g (7 oz) cooked prawns
1 baby gem lettuce, cut into 1 cm (½ in) pieces
1 tbsp snipped chives
1 tbsp chopped parsley
paprika to garnish

Sauce

2 tbsp tomato ketchup
1 tsp soy sauce
a few drops Tabasco
½ tsp Worcestershire sauce
75 ml (3 fl oz) double cream
4 tbsp mayonnaise
squeeze lemon juice

Cook the pasta according to the packet instructions. Mix together all the ingredients for the salad.

To make the sauce, mix together all the ingredients, adding the lemon juice to taste. Toss the salad with the sauce and sprinkle a little paprika on top.

Lunchbox lowdown
- Sometimes children like to eat breakfast for lunch – try packing some of your child's favourite cereal and a small carton of milk.

Cherub's couscous salad

Couscous is quick and easy to prepare and combines very well with chicken, vegetables and dried or fresh fruit. This couscous salad has a lovely crunchy texture because of the toasted sunflower seeds.

Makes 4 portions

40 g (1½ oz) chicken, cut into pieces (either cooked or raw)
300 ml (½ pint) chicken stock
2 tbsp sunflower seeds
100 g (4 oz) couscous
½ apple, peeled and grated
1½ tbsp freshly squeezed lemon juice
1 carrot, peeled and grated
1 small courgette, grated
1 spring onion, sliced

If you are not using cooked chicken, put the raw chicken into a saucepan with the stock, bring to the boil and then simmer for about 5 minutes or until cooked through.

Meanwhile, heat a dry frying pan and toast the sunflower seeds, continuously stirring for about 2 minutes or until lightly browned.

Remove the chicken from the stock and bring the stock back to the boil. Put the couscous into a bowl, pour over the stock and leave for 5 minutes to absorb the stock. Fluff up the couscous with a fork. Mix the apple with the lemon juice and stir into the couscous with the grated carrot, courgette, sunflower seeds and the spring onion.

Chef's salad with turkey & cheese

You can add other ingredients to this salad if you like:
- Add some cooked sweetcorn or cherry tomatoes.
- Include a boiled egg instead of the cheese.
- Replace the turkey with chopped sliced ham.

As an alternative dressing, mix mayonnaise with a little white wine vinegar or use the dressing that accompanies the Pasta with prawns & avocado recipe on the opposite page.

To make the dressing, whisk together all of the ingredients.

Mix together all the salad ingredients and toss in as much of the dressing as you like (there will probably be some dressing left over).

Makes 1 portion
Dressing
1 tsp red wine vinegar
½ tbsp runny honey
2 tbsp olive oil
1 tsp orange juice
salt and freshly ground
    black pepper

50 g (2 oz) cooked turkey,
    cut into cubes
4 cherry tomatoes, halved
⅛ cucumber, cut into cubes
½ baby gem lettuce,
    cut into pieces
50 g (2 oz) Edam cheese,
    cut into cubes
1 salad onion, finely sliced
½ punnet mustard and cress

Lunchbox lowdown
- According to a recent Mintel survey on lunchboxes just over 25% of lunchboxes contained no fruit or vegetables. Very few parents pack only healthy foods. However, the majority (65%) attempt to balance, giving children items such as chocolates or crisps but also giving fruit or vegetables. Almost three in ten mothers are 'sweet avoiders' who allow crisps and other savoury snacks, but do not give biscuits or chocolates.

Chicken salad with sweetcorn, pasta & cherry tomatoes

Makes 6 portions
2 chicken breasts
600ml (1 pint) chicken stock
100 g (4 oz) pasta bows,
  cooked and cooled
100 g (4 oz) canned or frozen
  sweetcorn
18 small cherry tomatoes,
  cut in half
2 spring onions, finely sliced
½ baby gem lettuce, shredded

Dressing
3 tbsp olive oil
1 tbsp white wine vinegar
½ tsp Dijon mustard (optional)
½ tsp sugar
salt and freshly ground
  black pepper
1 tbsp chicken stock from
  the poaching liquid

This is the most delicious, easy to prepare chicken salad. It's great for lunch or supper and is also good for a child's lunchbox. Pasta provides a good source of energy and if you add chicken or tuna, you get a good mix of complex carbohydrate and protein.

Poach the chicken in the stock for about 10 minutes, then leave to cool completely. Remove the chicken with a slotted spoon and cut into bite-sized pieces (this can be prepared the night before).

To make the dressing, whisk together all of the ingredients. Combine the rest of the ingredients for the salad with the chicken and toss in the dressing.

Makes 2–3 portions
Suitable for vegetarians
2 tbsp pine nuts
75 g (3 oz) baby spinach or
    mixed salad leaves
25 g (1 oz) peeled and diced red
    onion
1 small or ½ large ripe mango,
    peeled and chopped
5 strawberries, hulled and sliced
2 tbsp dried cranberries

Dressing
3 tbsp vegetable oil
1 tbsp balsamic vinegar
1 tsp sugar
salt and freshly ground black
    pepper

Spinach salad with mango & strawberries

This is a lovely combination of flavours, which is easy to prepare and very popular with my children. In fact, I often make it when I have friends over for supper. Mangoes are very rich in antioxidants. One average, sized mango provides the minimum adult daily requirement of vitamin C, two-thirds of the vitamin A and nearly half the vitamin E. Ripe mangoes are easy to digest and are also a good source of fibre.

Vitamin C boosts iron absorption, which can aid concentration. Vitamin E promotes normal cell growth and development and vitamin A helps boost the immune system, helps fight colds and infections and helps promote good eyesight.

Heat a dry frying pan and toast the pine nuts, continuously stirring for about 2 minutes or until lightly browned.

Meanwhile, combine all the ingredients for the salad in a bowl. Make the dressing by whisking together the oil, vinegar, sugar and seasoning. Then toss the salad with the dressing and sprinkle the pine nuts over the top.

Crunchy salad

As a child I used to love this salad. If you are short of time, you don't need to blanch the cabbage. You could also leave out the cabbage and simply mix grated carrot and raisins with the dressing.

Makes 1 portion
Suitable for vegetarians
50 g (2 oz) white cabbage, shredded
1 carrot, peeled and grated
1½ tbsp raisins

Dressing
2 tbsp mayonnaise
½ tbsp vegetable oil
1 tsp lemon juice

Blanch the cabbage in boiling water for 1–2 minutes and then drain. Using a fork, whisk together the ingredients for the dressing. Combine the cabbage, grated carrot and raisins and toss with the dressing.

Mixed salad

My children very much like this salad dressing, which is flavoured with soy sauce. You can add other ingredients like chopped chicken or turkey, avocado, toasted pine nuts or sunflower seeds.

Makes 1 portion
Suitable for vegetarians
25 g (1 oz) fine green beans, topped and tailed
50 g (2 oz) iceberg lettuce, cut into pieces
40 g (1½ oz) canned or cooked frozen sweetcorn
4 cherry tomatoes, cut in half

1 small carrot, peeled and grated
1 hard-boiled egg

Dressing
2 tbsp light olive oil
½ tbsp soy sauce
½ tbsp balsamic vinegar
a pinch of caster sugar
freshly ground black pepper

Blanch the cabbage in boiling water for 1–2 minutes and then drain. Using a fork, whisk together the ingredients for the dressing. Combine the cabbage, grated carrot and raisins and toss with the dressing.

Lunchbox lowdown
• Your child will probably only eat food that she feels comfortable eating in the school cafeteria. Most children are greatly influenced by peer pressure and just because your child likes eating raw cauliflower with a dip at home, she may not be comfortable eating this sort of food at school. So you have to find foods that suit your nutritional standards that are also acceptable among your child's social set.

Sweet
sensations

Nothing beats the taste of home-baked cookies and muffins and here
there are quick and easy recipes for children to make themselves for
their lunchboxes. To keep those lunchboxes looking healthy this chapter
also has many tempting recipes and ideas for fresh fruit.

Annabel's apricot cookies

These are my son Nicholas's favourite cookies. They are a rather unusual but totally irresistible combination of dried apricots, cream cheese and white chocolate.

Makes 18 cookies
Suitable for freezing
100 g (4 oz) unsalted butter
100 g (4 oz) cream cheese
100 g (4 oz) caster sugar
75 g (3 oz) plain flour
50 g (2 oz) chopped dried apricots
65 g (2½ oz) white chocolate chips or chopped white chocolate

Pre-heat the oven to 180°C/350°F/Gas 4.

In a large mixing bowl, cream together the butter and cream cheese. Add the sugar and beat until fluffy. Gradually add the flour, then fold in the apricots and chocolate. The dough will be quite soft – don't worry!

Drop the mixture by heaped teaspoons onto non-stick or lined baking sheets and bake in the oven for about 15 minutes or until lightly golden. Allow to cool and harden for a few minutes before removing them from the baking sheet and transfer to a wire rack.

Raisin & sunflower seed cookies

These are simple to make and taste better than any cookie you can buy. Raisins and sunflower seeds are packed full of nutrients and combine well with oats, which provide sustained energy. For a variation, add 40 g (1½ oz) chocolate chips.

Makes 14 cookies
Suitable for freezing
75 g (3 oz) butter
85 g (3½ oz) golden caster sugar
1 small egg, beaten
1 tsp vanilla essence
75 g (3 oz) raisins
50 g (2 oz) sunflower seeds
50 g (2 oz) plain flour
½ tsp bicarbonate of soda
½ tsp salt
40 g (1½ oz) porridge oats

Pre-heat the oven to 180°C/350°F/Gas 4.

Cream together the butter and sugar until light and fluffy. Beat in the egg and vanilla essence. Stir in the remaining ingredients until combined. Spoon tablespoons of the mixture onto non-stick or lined baking sheets, leaving enough space between the cookies for the dough to spread. Bake the cookies in the oven for 12–14 minutes until golden. Leave to cool for a few minutes and then transfer to a wire rack.

My favourite chocolate chip cookies

Makes about 36 cookies
Suitable for freezing

150 g (5 oz) soft brown
  sugar
100 g (4 oz) granulated
  sugar
100 g (4 oz) butter
100 g (4 oz) vegetable
  shortening
1½ tsp pure vanilla
  essence

1 egg
250 g (9 oz) plain flour
1 tsp bicarbonate of soda
½ tsp salt
175 g (6 oz) white or semi-
  sweet chocolate,
  broken into pieces
50 g (2 oz) sunflower
  seeds

Pre-heat the oven to 190°C/375°F/Gas 5.

In an electric mixer, cream together the sugars, butter and shortening and beat until light and fluffy. Add the vanilla and egg and blend well. Add the flour, bicarbonate of soda and salt and mix well. Stir in the chocolate and sunflower seeds. Line baking sheets with baking paper unless they are non-stick. Using floured hands, form the mixture into walnut-sized balls and place about 5 cm (2 in) apart onto the baking sheets.

Bake in the oven for 8–10 minutes until lightly golden. Leave to cool for a few minutes and then transfer to a wire rack.

Apple & carrot muffins with maple syrup

Makes 12 muffins
Suitable for freezing

125 g (4½ oz) wholemeal
  flour
50 g (2 oz) granulated
  sugar
25 g (1 oz) dried skimmed
  milk powder
1½ tsp baking powder
½ tsp ground cinnamon
½ tsp ground ginger
½ tsp salt

125 ml (4 fl oz)
  vegetable oil
3 tbsp maple syrup
1 tbsp honey
2 eggs, lightly beaten
½ tsp vanilla essence
1 large apple, peeled
  and grated
75 g (3 oz) carrots, peeled
  and grated
60 g (2½ oz) raisins

Pre-heat the oven to 180°C/350°F/Gas 4.

Combine the seven dry ingredients in a mixing bowl. In a separate bowl, combine the oil, maple syrup, honey, eggs and vanilla essence. Beat lightly with a wire whisk until blended. Add the grated apple, carrots and raisins to the liquid mixture and stir well. Fold in the dry ingredients until just combined, but don't overmix or the muffins will become heavy.

Line a muffin tray with paper cups and fill until two-thirds full. Bake in the oven for 20–25 minutes. Allow to cool for a few minutes, then remove the muffins from the tray and cool on a wire rack.

Mini chocolate chip muffins

Mini muffins are just the right size for little children and these ones are delicious. They are easy to make and fun for older children to make themselves.

Pre-heat the oven to 180°C/350°F/Gas 4.

Sift together the flour and cocoa and in a separate bowl cream together the margarine and caster sugar. Add the eggs to the creamed mixture, a little at a time, adding a tablespoon of the flour mixture with the second egg.

Mix in the remaining flour and cocoa until blended. Stir in the orange zest and chocolate chips. Line three mini muffin trays with paper cases and two-thirds fill each of the cases.

Bake in the oven for 12–15 minutes or until a toothpick comes out clean. Allow to cool for a few minutes, then remove the muffins and cool on a wire rack.

Makes 32 mini muffins
Suitable for freezing

125 g (4½ oz) self-raising flour
2 tbsp cocoa powder
125 g (4½ oz) soft margarine
125 g (4½ oz) caster sugar
2 eggs, lightly beaten
½ tsp grated orange zest
60 g (2½ oz) plain chocolate chips

Carrot & pineapple muffins

These are probably my favourite muffins. They are like miniature carrot cakes and are lovely and moist. You can make them with or without the icing.

Pre-heat the oven to 180°C/350°F/Gas 4.

Sift together the flours, baking powder, bicarbonate of soda, cinnamon and salt and mix well. In a separate bowl, beat the oil, sugar and eggs until well blended. Add the grated carrots, crushed pineapple, raisins and chopped pecans (if using). Gradually add the flour mixture, just beating until the ingredients are combined.

Pour the batter into muffin trays lined with paper cases and bake in the oven for 25 minutes. Allow to cool for a few minutes, then remove the muffins from the trays and cool on a wire rack.

To make the icing, beat the cream cheese together with the icing sugar. Split the vanilla pod and scrape out the tiny black seeds. Stir these into the icing and spread over the tops of the muffins.

Makes 12 muffins
100 g (4 oz) plain flour
100 g (4 oz) plain
   wholemeal flour
1 tsp baking powder
½ tsp bicarbonate
   of soda
1½ tsp ground
   cinnamon
½ tsp salt
200 ml (7 fl oz)
   vegetable oil
100 g (4 oz) caster sugar
2 eggs
125 g (4½ oz) finely
   grated carrots

225 g (8 oz) canned
   crushed pineapple,
   semi-drained
100 g (4 oz) raisins
40 g (1½ oz) chopped
   pecans (optional)

Cream cheese icing
175 g (6 oz)
   cream cheese
75 g (3 oz) sifted
   icing sugar
½ vanilla pod

Fruit smoothies

Fresh fruit smoothies are easy to make and chock full of vitamins from the fruit and calcium from the yoghurt. Older children will love making these themselves – all you need is an electric hand blender.

Mango, coconut & pineapple

Makes 2 glasses
125 ml (4 fl oz) coconut milk (from a can)
½ mango, peeled
125 ml (4 fl oz) pineapple juice
125 ml (4 fl oz) peach yoghurt drink
1 small banana

Combine all the ingredients together and purée in a blender until beautifully smooth.

Cranberry, raspberry & blueberry
Cranberries are rich in vitamin C – there is as much vitamin C in a glass of cranberry juice as there is in a glass of orange juice.

Makes 1 glass
75 g (3 oz) blueberries
75 g (3 oz) raspberries
150 g (5 oz) carton raspberry yoghurt or 125 ml
   (4 fl oz) raspberry drinking yoghurt
100 ml (3½ fl oz) cranberry and raspberry juice

Blitz all the ingredients together in a blender and strain through a fairly coarse sieve.

Peach melba

Makes 2 glasses
75 g (3 oz) fresh raspberries
½ x 425 g can peach slices in natural juice, drained
200 ml (7 fl oz) peach or raspberry flavoured drinking yoghurt
100 ml (3½ fl oz) milk

Purée together the raspberries and peaches and push through a sieve to remove the seeds. Using a hand blender, blend the yoghurt, fruits and milk until smooth.

Lunchbox lowdown
• You don't always have to give your child fruit juice in her lunchbox. A bottle of water is good – it's the most thirst-quenching drink and it won't spoil your child's appetite.

Exotic fruit, white chocolate & cereal cupcakes

These are quick and easy for children to make themselves and are a lovely treat for your child's lunchbox. Oats and dried fruits provide a good source of energy to keep your child going through the afternoon.

Makes 12 cupcakes

150 g (5 oz) porridge oats

50 g (2 oz) crispy rice

100 g (4 oz) mixed exotic dried fruits, e.g. papaya mango, pineapple, chopped

60 g (2½ oz) pecan nuts, chopped

100 g (4 oz) unsalted butter

125 g (4½ oz) golden syrup

85 g (3½ oz) white chocolate, broken into pieces

In a bowl, combine the oats, crispy rice, chopped exotic fruits and nuts. Put the butter, golden syrup and white chocolate into a saucepan and heat gently until melted. Stir the mixture into the dry ingredients until they are well coated.

Line a muffin tray with 12 paper cases and divide the mixture between them, pressing down lightly. Store in the fridge.

No-cook chocolate biscuit squares

This is a slight twist on the classic chocolate biscuit squares as I use ginger biscuits and crispy rice as well as digestive biscuits.

Makes 12 squares

75 g (3 oz) ginger biscuits
75 g (3 oz) digestive biscuits
100 g (4 oz) milk chocolate
100 g (4 oz) plain chocolate
100 g (4 oz) golden syrup
75 g (3 oz) unsalted butter
60 g (2½ oz) ready-to-eat dried apricots, finely chopped
40 g (1½ oz) raisins, cut in half
25 g (1 oz) crispy rice

Lightly grease and line a 20 cm (8 in) square shallow tin. Break the biscuits into pieces, place in a plastic bag and crush with a rolling pin until they are coarse crumbs.

Melt the chocolate, syrup and butter in a heatproof bowl over a pan of simmering water. Stir in the biscuit crumbs until well coated. Stir in the chopped apricots and raisins and finally stir in the crispy rice.

Spoon the mixture into the prepared tin, and level the surface by pressing down with a potato masher. Leave to cool, chill in the fridge for 1 hour and cut into squares.

Chocolate & apricot crispy rice squares

These are always popular and fun to make together with older children. They can also be made with white chocolate.

Makes 12 squares

75 g (3 oz) butter
100 g (4 oz) golden syrup
60 g (2½ oz) dark chocolate, broken into pieces
75 g (3 oz) crispy rice
75 g (3 oz) rolled oats
60 g (2½ oz) finely chopped dried apricots or mango or a combination of the two

Lightly grease and line a shallow 20 cm (8 in) square shallow tin. Put the butter, golden syrup and chocolate into a small saucepan and melt together over a low heat. Mix together the crispy rice, rolled oats and chopped apricots and stir into the golden syrup mixture.

Spoon the mixture into the prepared tin, and level the surface by pressing down with a potato masher. Leave to cool, chill in the fridge for 1 hour and cut into squares.

Lunchbox lowdown
• Communicate with your child, ask her what she enjoyed in her lunchbox. Look at what comes back untouched and ask without being defensive why it wasn't eaten and if there are any foods that other children bring to school that she would like to try.

Great ways with fruit

Every packed lunch should contain some fresh fruit. All fruit including dried fruit is a source of instant energy as well as containing lots of healthy nutrients. The natural sugars in fruit are easily digested for an instant power boost.

Fruit wedges

Children like to hold wedges of fruit so sometimes it's good to cut a variety of fruits into wedges and pack them in a plastic container with a lid. Wedges of pineapple, papaya and mango go well together and you could also include a kiwi fruit cut in half and your child can scoop out the flesh with a teaspoon. Good fruits for wedges are:

Mango	Peach
Pineapple	Papaya
Melon	Pear
Orange	Kiwi

Balls of fruit

Scoop out different coloured melon balls, e.g. ogen and cantaloupe melons, and add some black and white grapes. Galia melon works well too.

Fruit on a stick

Thread a selection of fruits onto a thin straw. You can use a mixture of fresh and dried fruits, e.g. kiwi, pineapple, grapes, strawberries and dried apricots.

Lunchbox lowdown
- Most children will leave food that takes a lot of effort to eat as they want a quick re-fuelling stop leaving maximum time for the playground. For example, give clementines already peeled and cover with cling film or cut kiwi fruit in half and let them scoop out the flesh with a teaspoon. Make sure your child can easily open his lunchbox and drinks container.

Quick & easy fruit salad

You can make delicious fruit salads using whichever fruits are in season. Peel and stone the fruit where necessary. I prefer to leave the skin on fruits like apples, plums and peaches as most of the vitamins lie just under the skin. Cut the fruit into bite-sized pieces and mix together with your chosen fruit sauce, two of which I've given here. The sauce adds to the flavour of the fruit salad and stops the fruit from discolouring.

Fruit salad
Cantaloupe and honeydew melon balls
1 kiwi fruit
½ mango, cut into chunks
1 thick slice pineapple, cut into chunks
1 clementine

Orange and lemon sauce
2 tbsp fresh squeezed orange juice
1 tbsp lemon juice
2 tsp caster sugar
1 passion fruit (optional)

Blackcurrant sauce
1 tbsp blackcurrant cordial
30 ml (1 fl oz) water
1 tbsp lemon juice
25 g (1 oz) caster sugar

To make the orange and lemon sauce, mix the juices and stir in the sugar until dissolved. If you like, add passion fruit seeds. For the blackcurrant sauce, mix the cordial, water and juice and stir in the sugar until dissolved.

Ruby red fruit salad

This is my favourite fruit salad. It has a wonderful flavour due to the rose water (you can buy this in large supermarkets) and the pomegranates add a crunchy texture that complements the berry fruits beautifully. This will keep for several days.

Makes 3 portions
1 large ripe peach
2 large red plums
20 g (¾ oz) butter
1½–2 tbsp caster sugar
1 tbsp rose water or orange flower water
(can also use plain water)
75 g (3 oz) raspberries
75 g (3 oz) blueberries
75 g (3 oz) blackberries
1 small pomegranate

Halve the peach and plums, remove the stones and cut each half of the plums into four pieces and each half of the peach into six pieces. Melt the butter in a large frying pan and place the plums and peach slices into the butter. Cook for 2 minutes before turning over and sprinkling with the sugar. Cook for a further 2–3 minutes and then pour over the rose water. Gently stir in the remaining fruits, including the seeds from the pomegranate, and heat through for approximately 1 minute. Leave to cool.

Lunchbox lowdown
- Don't give young children fruit with stones or they may choke.
- If you send a plum, peach or other squishy food in your child's lunchbox, wrap it in several layers of paper towels and then put it in a plastic bag.

Fresh berries with summer fruit coulis & yoghurt

Apple, plum & blackberry compote

Berry fruits are rich in vitamin C, which is a powerful antioxidant needed for growth and healthy skin and it also helps the body absorb iron from food. We cannot store vitamin C in our bodies so we need to eat vitamin C-rich foods every day. As a variation on this recipe, mix the fresh berries with the summer fruit coulis and leave out the yoghurt.

You can make delicious fruit compotes – try this mixed fruit version. Rhubarb or Bramley apples cooked with a little sugar until tender are also delicious. Compotes tend to taste best when using slightly tart fruit.

Makes 1 portion
100 g (4 oz) mixed frozen summer fruits, e.g. strawberries, raspberries, blueberries, blackberries, cherries and redcurrants

25 g (1 oz) caster sugar
100 g (4 oz) Greek yoghurt
100 g (4 oz) mixed fresh berries, e.g. blueberries, raspberries and strawberries

Makes 4–5 portions
1 large cooking apple, peeled, cored and chopped
4 plums, halved stoned and sliced

75 g (3 oz) caster sugar
1 vanilla pod or a pinch of cinnamon
125 g (4½ oz) blackberries

Make the fruit coulis by putting the frozen berries and sugar into a pan. Bring to the boil and simmer for 5 minutes. Purée in a blender.

Spoon the yoghurt into a plastic container together with the mixed berries and leave ready for your child to pour the fruit coulis over the yoghurt and berries at lunchtime.

Place the chopped apple, plums and sugar in a saucepan. Split the vanilla pod, scrape out the seeds and add these and the pod to the pan. Cover with a lid and cook for about 15 minutes. Add the blackberries, cover and simmer for a further 5 minutes. Remove the vanilla pod, leave the fruit to cool and then put the compote in the fridge to chill.

Lunchbox lowdown
• If your child wears a brace, avoid putting hard, crunchy foods like a whole apple in his lunchbox.

SWEET SENSATIONS

Index

Annabel Karmel

Annabel Karmel, the mother of three young children, is an international best-selling author of ten books and is a respected authority on child nutrition and childcare. She appears frequently on television and writes for national newspapers and magazines, including the *Times* and the *Sun* and is cookery expert for *Prima Baby* Magazine. Annabel is a celebrity chef and resident children's food writer on the BBCi website where she has created an extensive section on children's food. She has also designed children's food ranges for Marks & Spencer. For more information see www.annabelkarmel.com.

Acknowledgements

For the creation of this book my thanks go to Emma Callery, Grace Cheetham and Amelia Thorpe at Ebury, and Chris Shamwana, William Lingwood and Helen Trent.

The publishers and author would like to thank the following for their help: Mintel International Group Limited for their children's packed lunches report, Lakeland Plastics, John Lewis plc and Muji.